Liberty Savard

Fear Not AMERICA

Bridge-Logos *Publishers*

Gainesville, Florida 32614 USA

Fear Not America

Copyright © 2001 by Liberty Savard
Library of Congress Catalog Card Number: 2001098515
International Standard Book Number: 0-88270-8856

Bridge-Logos *Publishers*

P.O. Box 141630
Gainesville, FL 32614, USA
www.bridgelogos.com

DEDICATION

This book is dedicated to the heroes of the September 11th attack on America. Every rescue worker, firefighter, law enforcement officer, chaplain, medical volunteer, search and rescue volunteer, military volunteer, and patriotic volunteer who worked so hard—and the many still working—to help those who were lost and those who were saved.

This book is also dedicated to those who lost loved ones in the tragedy, and must now go on without them. I promise them that their loved ones did not die alone. Jesus was with them, comforting each one until their last breaths were taken. Not one of them stepped into eternity without being aware that the outstretched hand of Jesus was there for them.

TABLE OF CONTENTS

INTRODUCTION

This book is written to the American people who are working to go on with their lives in as normal a manner as possible, following the tragic terrorists' attack on America on September 11, 2001. Never before has America seen such a senseless and horrible loss of life and property at one moment in time.

I have attempted to give some perspective to what has happened, while assuring the reader that we have every reason to be filled with hope for the future. There is no reason to live in fear, for the one true God of all time and eternity is still in control. This is a time for great faith, but faith without any concrete understanding can be an extremely abstract concept for some to grasp when their emotions are supercharged with anxiety and fear. It is much easier to go through difficult times when you have some idea of what is going on and where God is in it.

Therefore, I have tried to answer the following questions in a concrete manner to give understanding and help dispel fears you may have about how this could have happened:

- **Was this God's judgment on America?**
- **Why did God allow this to happen?**
- **How will our leaders know what to do now?**
- **How do we live in victory with terrorism hanging over our heads?**
- **What is God going to do to the terrorists?**
- **What can we do about the biological warfare that may come?**

- **How can life go on as usual
  when we might die tomorrow?**
- **What can I do to encourage
  others?**
- **How should I pray?**

So that you might have understanding about the format of the prayers in this book, the following is a synopsis of the message that is the foundation of all of my books and teachings. Over 2000 years ago, Jesus said he was giving the Keys of the Kingdom, binding and loosing, to His people. He added this promise: *"Whatever you bind on earth will be bound in heaven, and whatever you loose on earth will be loosed in heaven"* (Matthew 16:19, *NKJV*). In this verse we find powerful prayer principles for bringing things on earth into alignment with God's already established will in heaven. Jesus himself prayed in the Lord's Prayer (Matthew 6:10; Luke 11:2), *"Thy will be done on earth as it is in heaven."*

Many Hebrew and Greek words for "bind" and "binding" have very positive meanings—tie, put oneself under obligation to, weave together, heal, undergird, hold, persuade, and cause fragmented pieces to coalesce and become one whole again. The word "loose" in the original Greek, *luo*, (and companion words *rhegnumi* and *agnumi*) mean untie, break up, destroy, dissolve, melt, put off, wreck, crack to sunder by separation of the parts, shatter into minute fragments, disrupt, lacerate, convulse with spasms, and tear up. These are strong words that a determined prayer warrior can accomplish great things with!

In Dr. Alfred Marshall's *Interlinear New Testament,*[1] J. B. Phillips states he was quite pleased that Dr. Marshall had not missed the peculiar Greek construction of Matthew 16:19. Phillips says this verse is not a celestial endorsement that God would bind and loose in heaven whatever we bound and loosed on earth. Rather, the keys in this verse are our means of coming into agreement with already established heavenly patterns. These principles of binding and loosing are our means of coming into agreement with God as we pray that His will, which has always been established in heaven, may now be manifested on earth.

As God's children, in prayer we can bind our wills to the will of God, bind our minds to the mind of Christ, and bind our souls to the truth of His Word. When we bind our wills to His, we are choosing to put ourselves under obligation to His plans and purposes. Praying with the binding key also brings God's power into the fight that your unsurrendered soul wages against Him for control of your life, helping begin the process of surrendering to Him.

In prayer we can loose our souls' ties to the old resentments, fear, and grave clothes they want to cling to. We can loose stronghold thinking, wrong mindsets, and the effects and influences of wrong agreements from our souls. Loosing prayers also wreak havoc with and cause spiritual terrorism on evil spirits, while destroying our souls' stronghold doors that the enemy accesses to harass us. Binding evil spirits is never effective if you do not deal with closing the soul's open doors of access in the soul. The spirits will just keep turning up and throwing spiritual bombs through the open doors. Binding evil spirits can actually be like mopping up around an overflowing toilet without ever shutting off the source of the water.

Authority, protection, and right standing in any area of life, natural or spiritual, can be severely hindered, <u>even rendered useless</u>, by the presence of open doors that an enemy can come and go through. Leaders in the armed forces of the U.S. will tell you that <u>their highest levels of authority and power are</u>

<u>useless</u> if there are open doors in their supply lines, communication systems, and battle planning rooms. There isn't a smart enemy alive who won't use those open doors to attack, slash, and burn—and the Christian's enemy is not stupid. Nor should we think that the terrorists are stupid, for a great deal of cunning and forethought went into their attack on America. It is never wise to underestimate your enemies!

These keys also offer a powerful way of praying for others. Some people struggle with praying to bind another person's will to the will of God—even calling it witchcraft. But ask yourself, what is the goal of witchcraft? Witchcraft's goal is always to gain power and benefit from controlling another person's will. If you pray and bind someone's will to the will of God, where is your gain of power or benefit? Binding someone's will to God's will and someone's mind to Christ's draws that person into a temporary, but powerful, closeness with the Father and the Son. They can pull away from this closeness at any time. But I believe that those who have been bound to the will of the Father and the mind of Christ will know that something was different, if only for a moment.

These keys create conditions within our souls that open us up to receive divine empowerment to accomplish the works God gives us to do. The Word is always *"effectually at work in you who believe—exercising its (superhuman) power in those who adhere to and trust in and rely on it"* (1Thessalonians 2:13, *AMP*). The binding and loosing prayers help us to come into that state of complete trust in God's Word.

Most of the people in the world today have no idea if any given Christian, Buddhist, Muslim, New Age believer, or Satanist is praying out of, making decisions by, or acting under the influence of a born-again human spirit linked with the Spirit of God. Some are praying under the influence of demonic spirits or the influence of the human soul. Christians pray, Buddhists pray, Muslims pray, New Agers pray, and Satanists pray. There is nothing "holy" in the act of just being a person who prays. The results from praying are based upon whom the prayers are prayed to and whether or not they are right prayers. God only involves himself in right prayers. I honestly believe there is only one basic "right prayer," which was the prayer of Jesus: *"Not my will, but your will be done, Father."*

To have true spiritual understanding of any person's, culture's, or religion's actions and words, you must be consistently <u>practicing and acting upon</u> what you have read in the Bible, while submitting to the Holy Spirit's guidance in response to your prayers. This kind of understanding belongs only to those *"whose senses and mental faculties are <u>trained by practice to discriminate and distinguish</u> between what is morally good and noble and what is evil and contrary either to divine or human law"* (Hebrews 5:14, *AMP*).

When people in an area are not in unity with the one true God, they often come into wrong agreements with others. Territorial spirits, principalities, and powers in high places find their access into or over geographical areas through the power released to them from the wrong agreements of the souls in the area. America, a country birthed out of many bold believers' desires to have freedom to worship God, has been filled with massive negative wrong agreements against God for decades.

Many peoples' groups have came into intensely wrong (in God's eyes) agreements in their souls. Hurt and hate has been carefully passed from generation to generation, creating new wrong agreements. Only when the effects and influences of these wrong agreements are loosed and destroyed will unbelievers begin to see their need for God.

The Word of God has given a battle plan to us in 2 Chronicles 7:14: *"If my people who are called by my name will humble themselves, and pray and seek my face, and turn from their wicked ways, then I will hear from heaven, and will forgive their sin and heal their land"* (*NKJV*). Only when this battle plan is followed in complete obedience and surrender will all people agree upon one prayer, one plea, one common cry, one unified hope: *"Not my will, not my religious denomin- ation's will, not my race's will, not my gender's will, not my culture's will, but THY WILL BE DONE, O LORD."* There is not really any other direction we can ever move towards in true unity.

We have an omniscient, omnipresent, omnipotent God who wants us to work in unity with Him in the healing of America. I believe He is saying something like this to each one of us:

"Fear not, America, for I am with you. I know exactly where every player is on the face of this earth at every moment. If you will cooperate with me, you will become a part of many of my Christians' finest hours. You

were born for such a time as this. The fields are ripe and ready for harvest, and many workers are needed to help them come into my Kingdom. Look to me, seek my face and my will, do what I say, and you will know victory at every turn. Do you trust me? Then get ready. If you do not fully trust me yet, then go back to my promises in my Word and read them over and over until you are ready. I'll be waiting for you."

PRAYER FOR AMERICA

Our Father in heaven, you have said that if your people would humble themselves and pray and seek your face and turn from their own wicked ways, then you would hear those prayers in heaven and heal our land. We humbly come to you, asking for your guidance and your grace to do what you say.

You have been merciful and long-suffering towards America. So many Americans have transgressed your law and turned away from you, refusing to give you place and honor within our schools, our government, and within our courts. Hear us, O gracious God, open your eyes and see the trouble of America. We do not make this request of you because we are righteous or deserving, but because of your great mercy. With repentance in our souls for our apathy towards you, we humbly acknowledge our need of you in this time of sorrow, fear, confusion, and the horror of war.

Your will must be the focus of all of our prayers from now on. Lord, I bind myself to your will and to the truth of your Word. I loose all human conclusions and soulish expectations out of my soul so that I might pray in agreement with your will.

Your Word says that requests, prayers, intercession, and thanksgiving should be made for all those in authority. We bind our President's will and all of his advisors' wills to your will, God. We bind their thoughts and plans to your timing. We loose all wrong counsel and the effects and influences of wrong agreements from every individual who has any part in directing the course of our nation right now.

We bind our leaders' minds to the mind of Christ. Remind them, Lord, that power without humility can be very dangerous. Let them submit to the words of wisdom spoken by the Holy Spirit. Whatever you speak to these leaders that you have given us to lead our country, we will support their decisions.

Our leaders have declared war. We do not rejoice in going to war, as war brings death to the innocent as well as to those who are wicked. But we must recognize that every person in America has been drafted into this war. Those who are headed overseas to fight in natural combat must be covered in prayer. If we are not on the front lines in person, then impress your people that we must be on the front lines in prayer. Lord God, we bind every military person, from the soldiers to the generals, to your will and purposes. We loose the enemy's assignments off of them. We bind their families to your will, and we ask that you would extend great grace and mercy and strength to each family member. We loose fearful and anxious thoughts from their souls.

We bind the government leaders of the nations of the world to your will and to the truth of your Word. We loose the hold of preconceived ideas and soulish conclusions from their minds, wills, and emotions. We loose the power and effects of the wrong agreements they have voluntarily made or felt coerced to make. We loose wrong counsel of others from them. We confess that your will shall be done in their lives, in their families, in their decisions, in their motives, and in their agendas.

You alone know what should be done, Lord. Thank you that you have given us a Christian president who openly confesses Jesus Christ as his Savior. The Word says that the king's heart is in your hand and you direct it like a river wherever you please. Please direct the heart of our President, and the hearts of his advisors.

Lord, many of us are struggling with wanting the terrorists to pay for their evil against innocent people. It is hard to ask that they might be forgiven and saved from the consequences of their sins, for they have done and continue to do so much harm. But you have said in your Word (Romans 12:19) that vengeance is yours. Lord, we acknowledge that we do not know what should be done here, for only you understand your plans for their lives.

As we pray for our leaders to hear your guidance, we ask that you would begin to supernaturally expose this network of terrorists. Lord, this enemy is not a country, or a race, or another religion. This enemy is hidden throughout so many nations of the world. You alone know where every member of this terrorist network is hiding. We ask that you apprehend them so that your will could be done in their lives. How your will should be accomplished in their lives is not up to us—so we just bind their wills to your plans.

We bind everyone associated with the terrorists to the will of God. We loose the enemy's assignments from them. We loose wrong cultural and religious bondage thinking from them, and we loose wrong beliefs and deceptions from them.

Holy Spirit, help us to not act or react in anger. Please move on the hearts of those who wish us harm, and change their hatred of us. Father, please give your protection and your grace and mercy to the innocent people in America and in other countries who may be attacked for looking Arab or for being Muslim. It is your desire for them to know your true love and your merciful care, too.

Lord, fear is stalking America right now. Fear of more attacks, of biological warfare, of loss of loved ones, even of dying. Fear is a strong, negative emotional reaction to tragic things that have happened, and it escalates rapidly when there are no guarantees that worse things are not yet coming. There is an antidote to all fears of more attacks,

*biological warfare, anthrax, and death—
it is faith in the promises in your Word.*

*Faith comes by hearing and knowing
the Word of God—the living words of
Jesus Christ. Remind us, and cause us to
remind each other, to seek out the
promises of your Word. We must fill
ourselves with the only all-purpose
antidote to mental and emotional fear.
Faith is trust and confidence in someone
or something. Lord, we will strengthen
our trust and confidence in you by
constantly feeding upon your words
written to us.*

*Thank you, Lord, for recording in your
Word that you did not turn Thomas or
Peter away from you when they
struggled with doubt and fear. I come to
you now for encouragement, strength,
and assurance so that I might cease my
struggles. I thank you for this moment
of rest in the present tense of your love
today. Right now, the past is over and the
future is not yet, and you are my
present-tense, right-now God.*

I bind myself to your timing for all things. I bind my mind to the mind of Christ, expecting an infilling of His thoughts and peace. I loose all wrong patterns of thinking that would try to set themselves against such an infilling. I loose all worries and anxieties over what has happened before and what will happen next.

Father, pour out your healing upon those who are mourning for lost loved ones. Please ease their pain and grief with your love. Reassure them that those who died in this tragedy were not alone when they took their last breath—Jesus was with each one of them. No one sat alone in any of the seats on the destroyed airliners. Jesus spoke with each one whether they knew Him or not. He offered them love, comfort, peace, and the opportunity to know Him. The people who collapsed in smoke-filled stairwells, unable to go any further— Jesus sat with them to the moment of their final breath, encouraging and comforting them.

The pilots, the flight attendants, the passengers, the people who worked in the buildings, the firemen, the chaplains, the policemen, the Christians, and the non-believers—not one of them died alone. Each one of them realized Jesus was with them before they died. Each one of them had the chance to take His hand and step into eternity with Him. The God who created time can turn an earthly millisecond into an hour of eternal understanding.

Lord, please do not let any religious, legalistic thinking close in on those left behind grieving. Not everyone gets saved at an altar in a church. Some get saved in airplanes, some in dark stairwells, and some in the millisecond before a disastrous event overtakes them.

The attack on America has been and is hard for human hearts to process and accept, Father. When this world closes in on me, let me remember to do what Jesus did—slip away and find a quiet place to pray. This is the only true and right response when I'm pushed beyond my finite limits. Help me to know when to reach out and pray with others, as strangers did all over America on September 11, 2001. If my circumstances prevent me from praying aloud during the day, please listen to my heart's quiet prayers for your will to be done.

Help all Americans to understand that money and power cannot guarantee security. Help them to seek first the Kingdom of God, loosing all fear and every doubt about whether or not you will be there for them. I loose all wrong beliefs, wrong teachings, wrong agreements, and wrong patterns of thinking from every person in America. I bind every person in this country to your will. Those who have felt the sting of prejudice or ignorance, those who have experienced strong emotional reactions because of being "different," Lord, I bind their minds to the mind of Christ. I loose the effects and influences of the negative agreements they have entered into with each other regarding the source of their pain.

Father, show us how to always pray in agreement for the one result that is always right: That your will would be done on earth as you have so set it in heaven. You have chosen us to be the instruments of what you want to manifest on earth. What an awesome responsibility you have entrusted us with and how we have fallen short of fulfilling it up until now. I will change!

What Satan meant for evil, Lord turn it to good. Let there be a great spiritual revival come from this tragedy—let many come to know Jesus Christ as their Savior and Lord. Amen.

What Has Happened?

Our Father in heaven, you have said that if your people would humble themselves and pray and seek your face and turn from their own wicked ways, then you would hear those prayers in heaven and heal our land. We humbly come to you, asking for your guidance and your grace to do what you say.

You have been merciful and long-suffering towards America. So many Americans have transgressed your law and turned away from you, refusing to give you place and honor within our schools, our government, and within our courts. Hear us, O gracious God, open your eyes and see the trouble of America. We do not make this request of you because we are righteous or deserving, but because of your great mercy. With repentance in our souls for our apathy towards you, we humbly acknowledge our need of you in this time of sorrow, fear, confusion, and the horror of war.

Your will must be the focus of all of our prayers from now on. Lord, I bind myself to your will and to the truth of your Word. I loose all human conclusions and soulish expectations out of my soul so that I might pray in agreement with your will.

The stage has been set for centuries for these last days and the perilous times that have now come upon us. God had His prophets write of these troubled days hundreds of years ago. He did not preordain them, but He knew that they would come. He knew that His people would not do what was necessary to prevent them from coming.

The Apostle Paul wrote to Timothy of these very days, *"But know this, that in the last days perilous times will come: For men will be lovers of themselves, lovers of money, boasters, proud, blasphemers, disobedient to parents, unthankful, unholy, unloving, unforgiving, slanderers, without self control, brutal, despisers of good, traitors, headstrong, haughty, lovers of pleasure rather than lovers of God, having a form of godliness but denying its power. And from such people turn away!"* (2 Timothy 3:1-5, *NKJV*).

Those days have come. But God's promise to us, from thousands of years ago until this very day, has always been the same. He would send His Son to offer life and hope and peace to every heart in the world. God has said that it was not His wish that any should perish, and His plans have never changed. *"The Lord is not slow in keeping his promise, as some understand slowness. He is patient with you, not wanting anyone to perish, but everyone to come to repentance"* (2 Peter 3:9, *NIV*). Jesus is coming back for those of us who will still be alive when He returns, while some are already home with Him. But everyone will have their chance to acknowledge and accept Him as their Savior and Lord.

Many have viewed September 11, 2001 as a day when the security and safety of our lives changed forever. Much of the world's inhabitants already knew that they were living in a far riskier time than Americans were aware of. The world did not really became more dangerous on that fateful morning, rather Americans were shocked into the reality of the danger already existing around us. The world was not as safe as we believed it to be before September 11, 2001, nor is it as dangerous as many now fear it to be.

Everyone has been given a reality check—believers and non-believers alike. It has been a shocking and sorrowful thing to view the horrifying pictures of the devastation of the terrorists' attack in New York. A catastrophe of this magnitude whiplashes our thoughts out of any self-comforting illusions that our mighty nation is untouchable. Who can deny the reality of the attack on America today?

Many Americans must now acknowledge one of the most important choices they will ever make: are they going to begin to live within God's will for their lives or are they going to continue to live outside of it by their own wits and self-wills?

Our God placed the answer and a plan for our land, and all other lands, in His Word centuries ago. We are told that if we will humble ourselves, pray, seek His face, and turn from our wicked ways, then He will hear our prayers and heal our land (2 Chronicles 7:14). We, who believe our God's words, must now begin to speak words of humility, pray right prayers, and seek to know Him rather than just asking Him for what He will give us. We must confess a true repentance and commitment to turn from our own wicked ways. Part of the original Hebrew meaning of the phrase "wicked ways" includes speaking negative words, causing others to feel pain, and being unjust.

From 9/11 to 911 to 91:1

When disaster strikes in America, Americans call 911. We are all beginning to recognize the state of emergency our country is facing, due to the technology available and the level of hatred within the sub-culture of radical terrorists around the world. Perhaps America has just had a 911 wake-up call regarding the days ahead. When was the last time a 911 operator called to warn you of impending danger?

I believe God wants us to remember that in addition to 9/11 and 911, there is yet a greater 91:1. Believers have long been comforted by Psalm 91, but now more than ever it can be the comfort of America. To make this beautiful Psalm completely understandable to anyone, please consider it in four scriptural versions at once. This is God's 91:1 to consider at this time.

PSALM 91

IN

King James Version
The Message
Amplified Bible
THE LIVING BIBLE

Verse 1:

He that dwelleth in the secret place of the most High shall abide under the shadow of the Almighty.

You who sit down in the High God's presence, spend the night in Shaddai's shadow.

He who dwells in the secret place of the Most High shall remain stable and fixed under the shadow of the Almighty whose power no foe can withstand.

WE LIVE WITHIN THE SHADOW OF THE ALMIGHTY, SHELTERED BY THE GOD WHO IS ABOVE ALL GODS.

Verse 2:

I will say of the LORD, he is my refuge and my fortress: my God; in him will I trust.

Say this: God, you're my refuge, I trust in you and I'm safe!

I will say of the Lord, He is my refuge and my fortress, my God, on Him I lean and rely, and in Him I confidently trust!

THIS I DECLARE, THAT HE ALONE IS MY REFUGE, MY PLACE OF SAFETY; HE IS MY GOD, AND I AM TRUSTING HIM.

Verse 3:

Surely he shall deliver thee from the snare of the fowler, and from the noisome pestilence.

That's right—he rescues you from hidden traps, shields you from deadly hazards.

For then He will deliver you from the snare of the fowler and from the deadly pestilence.

For he rescues you from every trap and protects you from the fatal plague.

Verse 4:

He shall cover thee with his feathers, and under his wings shalt thou trust: his truth shall be thy shield and buckler.

His huge outstretched arms protect you— under them you're perfectly safe; his arms fend off all harm.

He will cover you with His pinions, and under His wings shall you trust and find refuge; His truth and His faithfulness are a shield and a buckler.

He will shield you with his wings! They will shelter you. His faithful promises are your armor.

Verse 5:

Thou shalt not be afraid for the terror by night; nor for the arrow that flieth by day;

Fear nothing—not wild wolves in the night, not flying arrows in the day,

You shall not be afraid of the terror of the night, nor of the arrow, the evil plots and slanders of the wicked, that flies by day,

NOW YOU DON'T NEED TO BE AFRAID OF THE DARK ANY MORE, NOR FEAR THE DANGERS OF THE DAY,

Verse 6

Nor for the pestilence that walketh in darkness; nor for the destruction that wasteth at noonday.

Not disease that prowls through the darkness, not disaster that erupts at high noon.

Nor of the pestilence that stalks in darkness, nor of the destruction and sudden death that surprise and lay waste at noonday.

NOR DREAD THE PLAGUES OF DARKNESS, NOR
DISASTERS IN THE MORNING.

Verse 7:

**A thousand shall fall at thy side, and ten
thousand at thy right hand; but it shall not
come nigh thee.**

*Even though others succumb all around, drop
like flies right and left, no harm will even
graze you.*

A thousand may fall at your side, and ten
thousand at your right hand, but it shall not
come near you.

THOUGH A THOUSAND FALL AT MY SIDE, THOUGH
TEN THOUSAND ARE DYING AROUND ME, THE
EVIL WILL NOT TOUCH ME.

Verse 8:

**Only with thine eyes shalt thou behold and
see the reward of the wicked.**

*You'll stand untouched, watch it all from a
distance, watch the wicked turn into corpses.*

Only a spectator shall you be, yourself inaccessible in the secret place of the Most High, as you witness the reward of the wicked.

I WILL SEE HOW THE WICKED ARE PUNISHED, BUT I WILL NOT SHARE IT.

Verse 9:

Because thou hast made the LORD, which is my refuge, even the most High, thy habitation;

Yes, because God's your refuge, the High God your very own home.

Because you have made the Lord your refuge, and the Most High your dwelling place,

FOR JEHOVAH IS MY REFUGE! I CHOOSE THE GOD ABOVE ALL GODS TO SHELTER ME.

Verse 10:

There shall no evil befall thee, neither shall any plague come nigh thy dwelling.

Evil can't get close to you, harm can't get through the door.

There shall no evil befall you, nor any plague or calamity come near your tent.

HOW THEN CAN EVIL OVERTAKE ME OR ANY PLAGUE COME NEAR?

Verse 11:

For he shall give his angels charge over thee, to keep thee in all thy ways.

He ordered his angels to guard you wherever you go.

For He will give His angels especial charge over you, to accompany and defend and preserve you in all your ways of obedience and service.

FOR HE ORDERS HIS ANGELS TO PROTECT YOU WHEREVER YOU GO.

Verse 12:

They shall bear thee up in their hands, lest thou dash thy foot against a stone.

If you stumble, they'll catch you; their job is to keep you from falling.

They shall bear you up on their hands, lest you dash your foot against a stone.

THEY WILL STEADY YOU WITH THEIR HANDS TO KEEP YOU FROM STUMBLING AGAINST THE ROCKS ON THE TRAIL.

Verse 13:

Thou shalt tread upon the lion and adder: the young lion and the dragon shalt thou trample under feet.

You'll walk unharmed among lions and snakes, and kick young lions and serpents from the path.

You shall tread upon the lion and adder, the young lion and the serpent shall you trample under foot.

YOU CAN SAFELY MEET A LION OR STEP ON POISONOUS SNAKES, YES, EVEN TRAMPLE THEM BENEATH YOUR FEET!

Verse 14:

Because he hath set his love upon me, therefore will I deliver him: I will set him on high, because he hath known my name.

I'll give you the best of care if you'll only get to know and trust me.

Because he has set his love upon Me, therefore will I deliver him; I will set him on high, because he knows and understands My name, has a personal knowledge of My mercy, love and kindness; trusts and relies on Me, knowing I will never forsake him, no, never.

FOR THE LORD SAYS, BECAUSE HE LOVES ME, I WILL RESCUE HIM; I WILL MAKE HIM GREAT BECAUSE HE TRUSTS IN MY NAME.

Verse 15:

He shall call upon Me, and I will answer him: I will be with him in trouble; I will deliver him, and honour him.

Call me and I'll answer, be at your side in bad times; I'll rescue you, then throw you a party.

He shall call upon Me, and I will answer him; I will be with him in trouble, I will deliver him and honor him.

WHEN HE CALLS ON ME, I WILL ANSWER; I WILL BE WITH HIM IN TROUBLE AND RESCUE HIM AND HONOR HIM.

Verse 16:

With long life will I satisfy him, and show him my salvation.

I'll give you a long life, give you a long drink of salvation!

With long life I will satisfy him, and show him My salvation.

I WILL SATISFY HIM WITH A FULL LIFE AND GIVE HIM MY SALVATION.

Why Did God Let This Happen?

Many are asking, "Why did God allow this to happen?" Some are even saying that this terrible tragedy was God's judgment being poured out upon America. If your earthly father warned you over and over about the danger of ignoring the law of gravity and you stepped off a cliff over a rocky canyon, would you blame your father? If your mother warned you again and again about the danger of driving too fast, would you blame your mother if you had a bad accident? Not if you were in touch with reality.

Americans are quick to look for someone to blame for tragedies that could have been prevented. In *The Message* (Peterson's contemporary translation of the Scriptures), we read in John 9 about Jesus and His disciples seeing a man who was blind from birth. His disciples asked, *"'Rabbi, who sinned: this man or his parents, causing him to be born blind?' Jesus said, 'You're asking the wrong question. You're looking for someone to blame. There is no such cause-effect here. Look instead for what God can do (now).'"*

I do not believe that God caused the attack on America, nor do I believe it was God's judgment being poured out upon our country. God has richly blessed America, but God has always had some very specific laws set in place that firmly shape the boundaries of our lives on this planet.

- **For every action, there is a reaction.**
- **For every choice, there is a consequence.**
- **For every right agreement, God's power is present.**
- **For every wrong agreement, the power of darkness is released.**

This tragedy was a consequence of, as well as reaction to, many wrong actions, wrong choices, and wrong agreements that Americans have made. America has also allowed many of their leaders to make wrong choices. God often tempers some of life's more negative consequences with grace and mercy when a wrong choice has been genuinely believed to be right in His sight. But the corporate acts, choices, and agreements that have led up to the current situation America is now facing do not fit into any "believed to be right in His sight" category. Too many Americans, individually as well as corporately, have willfully chosen to do what they wanted, with no consideration for what God wanted.

This country, birthed over two hundred years ago out of a passionate desire for freedom to worship and personally know the one true God, now seems to have a passionate desire to ignore Him. Some may want Him around in crises, but wish to relegate Him to the outermost corner of their lives when things are going well. The negative consequences of such choices can very painful when endured without His grace and mercy—somewhat like surgery with no anesthesia.

When the Creator of all we are and all we know is pushed out of lives, He does not push His way back into those same lives to give grace for the resulting consequences. When God has been banned from our schools, banned from our halls of government, banned from our courts, and banned from so many other areas of the American life, the results are bound to be grave.

God has allowed America a glimpse of what life's consequences could be like if He continued to allow Americans to force Him out of their lives. No good father would allow his children to push him away when they were in very dangerous situations. A good father would do whatever was necessary to get their attention to protect them from further harm. This glimpse from the dark side of the consequences of our wrong choices is a wake-up call so that, as a nation, we can turn back to Him before it truly is too late.

OUR LEADERS

Your Word says that requests, prayers, intercession, and thanksgiving should be made for all those in authority. We bind our President's will and all of his advisors' wills to your will, God. We bind their thoughts and plans to your timing. We loose all wrong counsel and the effects and influences of wrong agreements from every individual who has any part in directing the course of our nation right now.

We bind our leaders' minds to the mind of Christ. Remind them, Lord, that power without humility can be very dangerous. Let them submit to the words of wisdom spoken by the Holy Spirit. Whatever you speak to these leaders that you have given us to lead our country, we will support their decisions.

Our government has declared war. We do not rejoice in going to war, as war brings death to the innocent as well as to those who are wicked. But we must recognize that every person in America has been drafted into this war. Those who are headed overseas to fight in natural combat must be covered in prayer. If we are not on the front lines in person, then impress your people that we must be on the front lines in prayer! Lord God, we bind every military person, from the soldiers to the generals, to your will and purposes. We loose the enemy's assignments off of them. We bind their families to your will, and we ask that you would extend great grace and mercy and strength to each family member. We loose fearful and anxious thoughts from their souls.

We bind the government leaders of the nations of the world to your will and to the truth of your Word. We loose the hold of preconceived ideas and soulish conclusions from their minds, wills, and emotions. We loose the power and effects of the wrong agreements they have voluntarily made or felt coerced to make. We loose wrong counsel of others from them. We confess that your will shall be done in their lives, in their families, in their decisions, in their motives, and in their agendas.

You alone know what should be done, Lord. Thank you that you have given us a Christian president who openly confesses Jesus Christ as his Savior. The Word says that the king's heart is in your hand and you direct it like a river wherever you please. Please direct the heart of our president, and the hearts of his advisors.

No human being on earth has the final answer right now. The best answers for what has happened and what we, as a nation, must do can only come from God. This is a time when all Christians should be praying harder than they ever have that God's will would prevail in the days and months ahead. He alone knows the souls of every person involved in every rocky road of this conflict, from beginning to end. Pray with fervor and faith, Christian, that our leaders will hear God's directives and sense God's timing. We must not be trying to second guess what our leaders are doing, nor question God about what is happening—but we must be praying that they would seek His will for every decision they make.

Jeremiah appealed to God (in Jeremiah 12) with his questions and concerns about why God was allowing the wicked to get away with so much. The prophet did not seem to be attempting to quarrel with God or find fault with His doing; rather he was pleading with God for understanding. We should never accuse or argue with our Maker, but we may reason with Him in order to have understanding *"'Come now, let us reason together,' says the LORD. 'Though your sins are like scarlet, they shall be as white as snow; though they are red as crimson, they shall be like wool. If you are willing and obedient, you will eat the best from the land; but if you resist and rebel, you will be devoured by the sword'"* (Isaiah 1:18-20, *NIV*).

The most mature Christian can be in the dark as to what God seems to be doing or allowing when difficult times come. We must ever be grateful that we have His permission to come boldly into His throne room to seek mercy, grace, and understanding regarding His ways. *"Let us then approach the throne of grace with confidence, so that we may receive mercy and find grace to help us in our time of need"* (Hebrews 4:16, *NIV*). He will give as much understanding as He knows that we need.

If we still do not understand and God does not speak further, we must always remember that He is God and His ways and His thoughts are higher than ours. We must know that He is righteous and always acts towards His people with love. Sometimes we just have to return to our most basic beliefs about Him and hang on when His choices seem hardest to understand.

It is nothing new to struggle to understand how the ways of evil people can succeed, causing good people and innocent people to suffer. In Jeremiah 12:2, the prophet spoke of evil people when he said to the Lord, *"You are always on their lips but far from their hearts. Yet you know me, O Lord, you see me and test my thoughts about you."* Could he have been thinking, "God, why aren't you watching them as closely as you are watching me?"

Jeremiah did not seem to consider that he might be facing worse trouble ahead—rather he was focusing upon God's current treatment of evil people. We read in verse 5 that the Lord rebuked Jeremiah's impatience, saying: *"If you have raced with men on foot and they have tired you out, then how can you compete with horses? And if you take to flight in a land of peace where you feel secure, then what will you do when you tread the tangled maze of jungle, haunted by lions in the swelling of the Jordan?"* (Jeremiah 12:5, *AMP*).

I think God was telling Jeremiah that if what he had faced up until then had so distressed him, while he was living in a land of peace and little danger—then what was he going to do when the Jordan River overflowed its banks and flooded the lions out of their thickets right into his front yard?

When God begins to correct us for being apathetic in our spiritual responsibilities to pray, He often starts with smaller trials designed to get our attention. How many smaller trials have we ignored as a country because America's milk and honey seemed to continue to flow to us whether we paid attention to God's warnings or not? And now, the lions have come out of their thickets and right into our front yards.

This attack on all that we have known and felt secure in may not be the biggest trial we are going to face. That is not to speak negatively, but to speak realistically. Whether worse times are coming or not, we can still know that God is fully aware and still in control. This takes the pressure off those who are continually seeking His face. His control is more than enough for us, <u>but He won't chase us down our self-guided paths to make us accept His help</u>. He will wait for us to turn and cry out to Him.

God is not wringing His hands wondering what to do; He's watching what we are going to choose to do. We need to begin renewing (or perhaps seeking for the first time) an up-close-and-personal acquaintance with the God who will bring us victoriously through whatever is flushed out of the thickets by this flood of evil.

God Has a Plan!

Let us begin to prepare for such an unknown future in useful ways, such as refusing to be downtrodden in our souls. The first step to accomplish this is to consider the makeup of our souls, so let's get personal. You and I have minds that need to be renewed, wills that need to be surrendered, and emotions that need to be divinely healed. This is because of the accumulation of sin and its effects and influences—pain, fear, anger—in our lives. We have been gathering soulish dirt and the crud of consequences throughout our whole lives. This is because we were born into this world without any spiritual link to the Spirit of our Creator in place. It is that very link that protects us and keeps us from being smothered under the world's gunk and junk.

Our original ancestors, Adam and Eve, sinned and broke man's spiritual link to the Spirit of God. Their disobedience severed their human spirit/Holy Spirit connection that they had enjoyed in the Garden of Eden. To fully experience God's love, mercy, grace, and divine direction today, our human spirits need to be reconnected to His Spirit. When we, by faith, request and accept the forgiveness that Jesus Christ purchased for us by His sacrificial death, a new spiritual birth occurs within us. We become born again into the Kingdom of God, forever spiritually connected to Him.

Unfortunately, most born-again Christians have accumulated enormous amounts of "stuff" in their souls by the time they become born again. This has come from dealing with the harsh cruelties of the world on human terms. Sad to say, the human soul does not give up its "stuff" when the human spirit gets born again, and the conflict begins. Once the honeymoon of the new believer and Jesus winds down a little, most new Christians wake up to find that they have a genuine war going on within themselves the born-again spirit versus the unsurrendered soul (or old nature).

The human soul does not take kindly to an omnipotent God showing up on the scene after the born-again experience, desiring to see all of the soul's personal secrets, power tactics, and control issues surrendered to Him. In fact, it reacts quite negatively to God's command to let go of all of its carefully documented injustices and abuses and just forgive everyone. Once again, although Christians' spirits have been born again, their minds, wills, and emotions were not renewed at the same time. The unsurrendered soul ferociously defends its right to continue hiding, revising, and chemically blotting out realities too harsh to handle, while simultaneously believing it is fighting a corporate takeover by God.

Christians who are already struggling just to get through their everyday living can be thrown for a real knock down when they begin to believe that the American government's protection is only part-time. The rest of this book is about removing the deception and denial your soul has held onto in the belief that it, another human soul, or any government structure could protect you from the consequences of ignoring God. This soulish house cleaning is necessary to make room to receive the supernatural power inherent in the Word for those who will believe. Are you ready to believe and receive?

In prayer, we can bind our mind to the mind of Christ, that we might think in agreement with the thoughts He is thinking towards us—<u>especially at this time</u>. We can loose all preconceived ideas we have about ourselves, about God, about those around us, and about our enemies. We can loose fearful thoughts and break up their recycling program in our mind. Wouldn't you like to get rid of fearful thoughts instead of allowing your soul to just keep processing them over and over? By the words of our own mouths, we can pray and loose doubtful thoughts about God that would tear at our faith in His plans and purposes for us. Pray like this:

> ***Lord, according to your Word, I now bind my mind to the mind of Christ. I***

bind myself to the truth of your Word. I will dig deeper in your Word that I might have your truth within me, supernaturally working to steady my thoughts. I loose all wrong thoughts and preconceived ideas I have about myself, about you, and about those I consider to be my enemies. I loose all doubtful thoughts, all negative thoughts, and all worried thoughts my soul wants to obsess over. I am choosing your thoughts and your purposes from now on!

In prayer, we can bind our not-yet-surrendered wills to the will of God. Our wills appear to be the enforcers of our souls. They are control-bound, bulldog-related, aggressive enforcers, providing power to force the accomplishment of whatever the mind decides must be done. Our unrenewed minds assess nearly all situations within the framework of our unresolved issues. Current circumstances become linked, as if by fire, to past situations where we felt abandoned, rejected, or betrayed—where we felt that no one cared what happened to us. Fear floods in, and the mind frantically decides that something must be done—NOW! The will kicks in with its self-drive, soul power, and force necessary to accomplish the mind's directives–whether the mind's conclusions were right or wrong.

When the unsurrendered soul (of both the believer and non-believer) goes into overload as so many souls have done in the past few weeks, the mind doesn't know the answers. The emotions either flame out of control or become frozen in fear, and the will has no directive to enforce. These individuals are in a state that is a perfect set-up for outside control.

Who will reach them first? Will it be individuals with strong personal soul power, perhaps like Jim Jones or David Koresh, who see an opportunity to control and use them? Will it be demonic forces who know how to access the open doors of a soul on overload to control and abuse them? Or, will it be God?

The unsurrendered will is in danger when it surrenders to another human soul. It is also in danger when it becomes obstinate and stubborn.

Psalms 75:5 tells us that God has said this about the self-will *"Do not lift up your horn on high; do not speak with a stiff neck"* (*NKJV*). The word "horn" as used here means your soul's will-power and determination—the phrase "stiff neck" refers to stubbornness, rebellion, and rigidity in the soul. Matthew Henry's commentary gives us further understanding about what God is saying in this verse about being strong-willed, proud, and self-determined:

"Lift not up the horn; boast not of your power and prerogatives; persist not in your contumacy and contempt of the government set over you; lift not up your horn on high, as though you could have what you will and do what you will; speak not with a stiff neck, in which is an iron sinew that will never bend to the will of God in the government; for those that will not bend shall break; those whose necks are stiffened are so to their own destruction."[2] A strong self-will is not a good thing unless its strength is surrendered to the will of God. To begin to force your will to surrender, pray like this:

> *I bind my will to your will, Father. I know that my soul wants to make the choices of my life, but you alone have the understanding and knowledge of all things that are necessary to make right and godly choices. I bind my will, as well as my hands and my feet, to your plans and purposes for my destiny. I choose to do this so that I might walk and work*

according to your directives and your guidance. I loose my will's stubbornness, I loose its rigidity, and I loose its arrogance and determination to have the last say. I am choosing your way and your will from now on.

In prayer, we can bind our emotions to the comfort and healing of the Comforter, the Holy Spirit. Emotions appear to be the God-given spices and flavorings of our personalities that are different from our verbal and physical means of communicating. Without words and without movement, intense emotions can wash across a person's face, communicating a powerful understanding of exactly what is going on inside that person's soul. Joy is an emotion, excitement is based in the emotions, and peace is directly affected by our emotions. Who has ever mistaken the bright glow of joy on a face, the excited light of love in someone's eyes, or the serenity of a soul at peace?

However, emotions also come in darker colors that communicate themselves just as clearly. Anger is an emotion given by God to provide backup support to a surrendered will's courage and boldness. But this powerful emotion can turn very negative when someone

46

or something pushes an emotional hot-button or unhealed traumatic memory. Hatred and rage are angry emotions that have spun so far out of control, they can become deadly.

Fear is a powerful negative emotion, and its ability to trigger adrenaline can prompt a quick natural fight or flight response to potential danger. Fear is never part of a spiritual response to potential danger, however. Fear is not an evil spirit, but it happens to be a favorite point of involvement for demonic activity. Fear, hatred, and rage are always entangled with a person's unresolved issues, unhealed hurts, and unmet needs.

Many people have grown up uncertain about whether or not anyone cared enough to protect them. Many have grown up being told, "You got yourself into it, now get yourself out of it." Or, "Stop feeling sorry for yourself and deal with it." Or, "Terrible things happen to lots of people, get over it." Children are teased and taunted in schools; they are bullied and physically abused. Gangs are killing each other. Domestic violence is tearing the fabric of the family apart.

Where is the protection? We are a nation of people who have never been sure who or what is supposed to protect us. Government? Guns? Gangs? God? If only everyone knew just what He actually did for each one of us, we might receive and know His protection and nurturing love. If you have not experienced these gifts from Him, perhaps your first thoughts in stressful times are filled with anxiety and fear. God has been waiting to give you a permanent knowing that He is right there with you, so that your first thoughts always go right to Him.

THE TERRORISTS

As we pray for our leaders to hear your guidance, we ask that you would begin to supernaturally expose this network of terrorists. Lord, this enemy is not a country, or a race, or another religion. This enemy is hidden throughout so many nations of the world. You alone know where every member of this terrorist network is hiding. We ask that you apprehend them so that your will could be done in their lives. How you should do this is not up to us; therefore, we submit our wills to your will and ask that you would bring everyone into alignment with your plans.

We bind everyone associated with the terrorists to the will of God. We loose the enemy's assignments from them. We loose wrong cultural and religious bondage thinking from them, and we loose wrong beliefs and deceptions from them.

Holy Spirit, help us to not act or react in anger. Please move on the hearts of those who wish us harm, and change their hatred of us. Father, please give your protection and your grace and mercy to the innocent people in America and in other countries who may be attacked for looking Arab or for being Muslim. It is your desire for them to know your true love and your merciful care, too.

The terrorists' attacks on our country have produced reactions ranging from shock to grief to anger to war. Americans are not a particularly patient people. We prefer sound bites, microwaves, and instant answers. Our leaders have warned that this war on terrorism will not have a quick resolution. This has not been a war declared on a country or an individual, though it may seem so. The human enemy here is a network of terrorist groups that may span, as reported by various news media, more than fifty countries.

We could liken this to trying to surgically excise a rapidly spreading cancer. No sooner do you clean out one area of cells, than another area of cancerous cells in the body begins destroying good cells. Surgery on that area may seem successful, only to find out the cancer cells are established in still yet another area of the body. Is there any treatment or antidote that can actually stop the spreading of this worldwide terrorist network? Yes, there is. But it may "cost" more than most Americans are willing to pay. More about that later.

It has been interesting to read that the classic terrorist scenario is not to try to take over a country by superior force, but to make a country's citizens become fearful. They then lose faith in their government and doubt their leaders, which causes the unity of the people to be dissolved, leading to the nation's demise. This has been the strategy over the past century in many different terrorist hot spots in the world. Whether the attempts to overthrow a government by demoralizing a nation's faith in their leaders works or fails, damage is always done.

Be very aware of the emotionally overheated, baseless speculating, and nerve twitching outpouring of "news" stories and rumor debating now permeating our media. In the first days after the terrorists' attack, the television networks seemed to be trying very hard to handle the collective sharing of national shock. The major network anchors all seemed to rise to the occasion with leadership and sensitivity. Now, much of the media seems to be ignoring the fact that they are fanning fires of terror and panic across the country in an attempt to keep the nation's attention.

It is ironic that the media is sensationalizing so much of the "breaking" news (over and over and over), when the public is hungering for a deeper perspective and understanding of what is really happening. Each of us knows that when we have seen a "live" news report for the fifth time, we begin to tune it out. I believe this hunger for a deeper perspective will cause many to seek the face of God. Christians must be prepared to respond to that seeking, but not to try to force it to happen.

Pray for media leaders to realize that they have a duty to not play into the terrorists' plans of damaging the national spirit of Americans. The media must not cooperate with the terrorists who hijacked our airplanes by feeding into their desires to demoralize America through a surrogate hijacking of our airwaves as well. Pray like this:

> *Lord, I bind the wills of all of the media people to your will. I bind their minds to the mind of Christ, that His thoughts can temper their decisions. I bind them to the truth, that they will not be tempted to exaggerate. I loose wrong counsel from them, and I loose the effects and influences of the words from their superiors that would drive them to sensationalize the truth. I loose the greedy, needy patterns of thinking that would cause them to be unwise. The journalists, newscasters, and radio talk show hosts hold a very important role in our nation. Guide them to think responsibly and with sensitivity.*

I believe our President and our leaders have been right with their encouragement of Americans to get back to life as usual. We must not allow threats and rumors to disrupt our lives to the point that people begin to withdraw from the daily fabric of a healthy albeit cautious society. When warnings and alerts come about the possibility of more attacks, yet no details or instructions are given, Christians must immediately go to their knees and pray for God to give wisdom and direction. Christians need to pray that Americans do not develop a "you cried wolf too many times" attitude towards such warnings. This type of attitude could be the very goal of the terrorists as they release information about further attacks. What better time for a devastating and demoralizing attack than when people have decided nothing is going to happen?

Christians must realize that their God-given ability to rise above shock, grief, and fear is an opportunity to become spiritual leaders at a grass roots level. If you are a believer, yet you are still reeling with shock and fear, keep reading. If you are not a believer and you are struggling with shock and fear, keep reading.

I was asked if I wanted to write a nice encouraging book on comfort for these times. I could not, for I do not believe we need to have our hands held and faces patted right now. I was asked if I wanted to write something that even non-believers and nominal Christians would be comfortable reading. I have not done this. This book is written to the meat-eating Christian, the strong warrior believer who wants to spiritually pull down the territorial strongholds and principalities that have set up domains over this country. This book is written to the Christian who wants to be a life-changer, the one who wants to boldly make a difference in our nation's future.

The Mystery of Iniquity

The Lord said in Zechariah 1:15, *"I am very angry with the nations that feel secure. I was only a little angry, but they added to the calamity" (NIV)*. Matthew Henry's commentary paraphrases God's words like this: "'I was but a little displeased with <u>my people</u>, and designed to correct them moderately, but those that were employed as instruments of the correction cast off all pity, and with the greatest rage and malice helped forward their affliction and added to it.' . . . God is displeased with those who help forward affliction even of those who suffer justly."

I believe God may have allowed us this small glimpse of life as it would be <u>without</u> the blessings and protection that He has poured out upon America for so long. However, those who moved in to take advantage of the opportunity went over the line God had drawn. God's justice for those who take innocent life is far above any type of human justice we might try to mete out.

The Apostle Paul spoke in 2 Thessalonians 2:7 of the mystery of iniquity or the secret of lawlessness. Matthew Henry's Commentary tells us that this mystery of iniquity (as identified by Paul in the above verse) was manifested in "wicked designs and actions concealed under false shows and pretenses, at least they were concealed from the common view and observation. <u>By pretended devotion, superstition and idolatry were advanced; and, by a pretended zeal for God and His glory, bigotry and persecution were promoted</u>." The terrorists who attacked America profess intense religious devotion. Through their pretended zeal for God, persecution, torture, and murder are being promoted as righteous. They are pouring out of the wrath of man upon those they hate, hiding behind the pretense of a holy war, but there is nothing "holy" about what has happened.

Psalm 76:10 (*KJV*) tell us that *"surely the wrath of man shall praise thee: the remainder of wrath shalt thou restrain."* We do live in an angry world where we often feel the wrath of man. But as far as God permits the wrath of man to break forth at any time, we have the promise that man's wrath is useless when it has outlasted its allowed window of opportunity and God restrains it. Some of God's redeemed people went home in the 9/11 tragedy. We don't know why. The intricacies of His plans and purposes for each of our lives must be left up to Him in His timing, which is always filled with grace and mercy as well as eternal purpose.

America has long been blessed with His protection because America was birthed out of courageous believers' desires to be able to worship God freely, and to have life, liberty, and be able to pursue true happiness. However, America has drawn too many soulish and selfish inferences from the meaning of the pursuit of happiness—believing that happiness comes from self-established rights, excessive power, soulish control, and greed. In the terrorists' attacks, is it not possible that God could be saying to Americans, *"Are you sure you really want to continue living your lives without my protection, my guidance, and my rules that were set in place to keep you safe and truly happy?"*

This could be one of Christianity's finest hours in modern times. At such a time as this, most Americans became aware that Christianity was never meant to be just a label—nor was Christianity ever meant to be God's army reserves to be called up only when there is a crisis. I believe there is a greater awareness in America now that God's people have been right—He is the rock to stand on and the strong hand to hold.

A truly fearless faith has no problem understanding the truth of God's Word about the coming days. I appreciate how Peterson addresses 2 Timothy 3: 1-5 in *The Message:*

"Don't be naïve. There are difficult times ahead. As the end approaches, people are going to be self-absorbed, money-hungry, self-promoting, stuck-up, profane, contemptuous of parents, crude, coarse, dog-eat-dog, unbending, slanderers, impulsively wild, savage, cynical, treacherous, ruthless, bloated windbags, addicted to lust, and allergic to God. They'll make a show of religion, but behind the scenes they're animals. Stay clear of these people."

This perfectly describes the minds of the terrorists. Basically, we thought we were clear of these terrorists, yet we were not. This is because America has become allergic to God's interventions in our daily lives. Proverbs 29:1 tells us this: *"For people who hate discipline and only get more stubborn, there'll come a day when life tumbles in and they break . . . "* (*TM*). We must turn around and embrace the rules God has laid down for our protection. The best laid plans of our leaders, in their own finite thinking without divine input, cannot protect us if our covering of the protection of God has been pushed back from us.

ANTIDOTE TO FEAR

Lord, fear is stalking America right now. Fear of more attacks, of biological warfare, of loss of loved ones, even of dying. Fear is a strong, negative emotional reaction to tragic things that have happened, and it escalates rapidly when there are no guarantees that worse things are not yet coming. There is an antidote to all fears of more attacks, biological warfare, anthrax, and death— it is faith in the promises in your Word.

Faith comes by hearing and knowing the Word of God—the living words of Jesus Christ. Remind us, and cause us to remind each other, to seek out the promises of your Word. We must fill ourselves with the only all-purpose antidote to mental and emotional fear. Faith is trust and confidence in someone or something. Lord, we will strengthen our trust and confidence in you by constantly feeding upon your words written to us.

Americans have rejected so much of the order of God, the rules of God, saying that they are too restrictive and not for everyone. Unfortunately, the rules they have rejected are the very rules that would keep them safe within God's plans. It is interesting that some of God's rules, immutable laws actually, cannot be rejected. Three such rules of God are the law of gravity, the power of agreement, and the inevitability of consequences.

Let us consider the most visibly obvious rule of God's making which is gravity. No matter who, why, where, when, or how something is dropped, the law of gravity takes over and it falls to the earth. This is a law that no one in his or her right mind would argue with. We should realize that all of God's laws have consequences. Get on the wrong side of them, and you can fall.

The law of agreement is just as true as the law of gravity. Any agreement occurring between souls, whether those souls are human or demonic, produces effects and influences that can be far reaching. I believe that demons do have souls, as a soul is composed of a mind, a will, and emotions. Demons do seem to have the ability to think, they seem to have the ability to make choices, and they certainly seem to have the ability to become angry and hateful.

One of the results of wrong agreement can be a mob mentality. Matthew 27:25 records the outcome of the fact that the Jewish mob outside of Pilate's palace were in one agreement. As they screamed at Pilate to pronounce the sentence of crucifixion upon Christ, Pilate tried to disassociate himself from the responsibility of such a sentence. He ceremonially washed his hands in water, a Greek and Hebrew custom expressing one's innocence of any guilt in a matter. As Pilate called out to the crowd that he was innocent of the blood of this man, the mob mentality of their wrong agreement burst forth in these words, " . . . *his blood be on us, and on our children"* (Matthew 27:25, *KJV*).

Adam Clarke's commentary on this Scripture is very revealing. He says that the people really were saying, "If this man be innocent, and we put him to death as a guilty person, may the punishment due to such a crime be visited upon us, and upon our children after us! What a dreadful imprecation and how literally fulfilled! The notes at Matthew 24 will show how they fell victims to their own imprecation, being visited with a series of calamities unexampled in the history of the world. They were visited with the same kind of punishment; for the Romans crucified them in such numbers when Jerusalem was taken, that there was found a deficiency of crosses for the condemned, and of places for the crosses. Their children, or descendants, have had the same curse entailed upon them, and continue to this day to be a proof of the innocence of Christ, the truth of His religion, and of the justice of God."[3]

When human souls get involved in wrong agreements, the power of darkness always moves in and ratchets up the stakes involved. In fact, I believe that demonic spirits feed off of corporate negative wrong agreements made by humans. In the book of Daniel, while the

Jewish people were in captivity in Babylon, they were grumbling, murmuring, and constantly coming into negative wrong agreements about God, His prophets, and their circumstances. It wasn't until Daniel began to pour his heart out in confession of his sins and the sins of his people that an answer was dispatched from heaven. Because Daniel was deeply distressed by the desolation of his people, he threw his soul upon the mercies of Almighty God:

"I turned to the Lord God and pleaded with him in prayer and petition, in fasting, and in sackcloth and ashes. I prayed to the LORD my God and confessed: O Lord, the great and awesome God, who keeps his covenant of love with all who love him and obey his commands, we have sinned and done wrong. We have been wicked and have rebelled; we have turned away from your commands and laws . . . Lord, you are righteous, but this day we are covered with shame . . . shame because we have sinned against you . . . all this disaster has come upon us, yet we have not sought the favor of the LORD our God by turning from our sins and giving

attention to your truth . . . Now, our God,
hear the prayers and petitions of your
servant . . . We do not make requests of
you because we are righteous, but
because of your great mercy. O Lord,
listen! O Lord, forgive! O Lord, hear and
act! For your sake, O my God, do not
delay, because your city and your people
bear your Name"
            (Daniel 9:3-19, *NIV*).

    Read this entire passage in your Bible to
see how broken Daniel was in his confession.
While he was still in prayer, the archangel
Gabriel came to him in swift flight, telling
Daniel that he had come to give him insight
and understanding. Gabriel said that as soon as
Daniel had begun to pray this prayer, the
answer was given and he had been dispatched
to bring it with understanding. In Daniel
10:12, we read that since the first day Daniel
had set his mind to gain understanding and
humble himself before God, his words were
heard and Gabriel had come in response to
them. But the prince of Persia had resisted him
for twenty-one days. The archangel Michael
was sent to help him, and Gabriel was finally
able to get through to Daniel.

The prince of Persia was a territorial spirit who had dominion over the area of Babylon and beyond. I believe it had been feeding off the wrong agreements the Israelites were continually making against God. Hundreds, perhaps thousands, of Israelites caused this problem. Yet it only took one man to get it right. One man stood up and confessed his sins against God, as well as confessing that his people had also sinned and rebelled against God. That confession caused two archangels to be dispatched from heaven to take out the prince of Persia. That had to be one bad territorial spirit, that Gabriel alone could not get him down. Yet it only took the prayer of the right heart of one man, Daniel, to set the answer in motion.

Right agreements always result in God's power being established in circumstances and lives. Wrong agreements always result in darkness and evil being established in circumstances and lives. If we flirt with the law of gravity by dancing on the edge of a cliff and we fall off—frantic prayer will not stop us from being smashed into oblivion at the foot of that cliff. We will pay the price for ignoring the consequences of the law of gravity. We must not flirt with words of wrong agreement and expect to ignore their consequences. We are better off to be silent than create darkness and evil with our words. Pray like Daniel did and pray like this:

> *I bind my will to your will, Lord, and I commit myself to praying in agreement with the Word. Your Word tells me that you sought a man among the many who should build up the wall and stand in the gap before you and the land you were about to judge (Ezekiel 22: 30). Lord, I want to stand in the gap for my land, America. I have sinned against you and my nation has sinned against you, but I ask for your forgiveness, your grace, your mercy, and your favor upon all of the people of America. Deliver us from our sin and its consequences. Over and over your Word shows that you have sent a man or a woman to stand between your righteous judgment and those who deserved to be judged. All you need is one person to truly intercede and pray for your will to be done in peoples' lives. Dear God, here I am: Ready and willing to intercede and pray–to plead for forgiveness and mercy for America's people.*

Faith Versus Fear

Fear is an emotional reaction to a traumatic circumstance–actual or perceived. We've all had traumatic things happen to us, and we often struggle with our feelings about them. Yet Jesus echoed the Father in saying that we should fear not. He did not say that we should try not to worry, or that we should hope that we wouldn't become afraid. He said, *"Fear not, little flock; for it is your Father's good pleasure to give you the kingdom"* (Luke 12:32, *KJV*).

The Bible is full of "fear nots," both in the Old and the New Testament. God has repeated himself about this issue of fear, a very powerful negative human emotion, all through the Bible. In the *King James Version* of the original manuscripts, the Lord has said <u>fear not</u> at least 47 times in the Old Testament and 15 times in the New Testament.

"Don't worry about anything; instead, pray about everything; tell God your needs, and don't forget to thank him for his answers. If you do this, you will experience God's peace, which is far more wonderful than the human mind

can understand. His peace will keep
your thoughts and your hearts quiet and
at rest as you trust in Christ Jesus"
(Philippians 4:6-7, *TLB*).

Most of God's commands that include "fear not" are linked with the assurances of God being for us, being with us, encouraging us, and promising His help to us. Pray and thank God for His faithfulness and His goodness, agreeing with others about the loving character of God, while reading His promises in the Word. In prayer, loose your soul's self-defense systems that are withstanding Him. This allows Him voluntary access to get to your pain and fear. This is how you begin to cooperate with your own healing.

Faith is translated in numerous places in the Word, both in Hebrew and Greek, from words that mean "trust and confidence in the goodness and power of God towards you." Fear is a lack of "trust and confidence in the goodness and power of God towards you." Fear is also an emotional response to situations that remind us of frightening unresolved issues from when we felt helpless. Here are a few of God's assurances that He is on your side, and He is at your side.

1. *"Do not be afraid; do not be discouraged"*
    (Deuteronomy 1:21, *NIV*).

2. *"Don't be afraid, for the Lord will go before you and will be with you; he will not fail nor forsake you"*
    (Deuteronomy 31:8, *TLB*).

3. *"Yes, be bold and strong! Banish fear and doubt! For remember, the Lord your God is with you wherever you go"*
    (Joshua 1:9, *TLB*).

4. *"This is what the LORD says to you: Do not be afraid or discouraged because of this vast army. For the battle is not yours, but God's"*
    (2 Chronicles 20:15, *NIV*).

5. *"After I looked things over, I stood up and said to the nobles, the officials and the rest of the people, 'Don't be afraid of them. Remember the Lord, who is great and awesome, and fight for your brothers, your*

71

sons and your daughters, your wives
and your homes'"
    (Nehemiah 4:14, *NIV*).

6. *"The Lord is my light and my
salvation; whom shall I fear or
dread? The Lord is the refuge and
stronghold of my life, of whom shall
I be afraid?"*
    (Psalm 27:1, *AMP*).

7. *"He is my strength, my shield
from every danger. I trusted in him,
and he helped me. Joy rises in my
heart until I burst out in songs of
praise to him. The Lord protects his
people and gives victory to his
anointed king"*
    (Psalm 28:7-8, *TLB*).

8. *"God's love is meteoric, his
loyalty astronomic. His purpose
titanic, his verdicts oceanic. Yet in
his largeness, nothing gets lost, not
a man, not a mouse slips through the
cracks"*
    (Psalm 36:5-6, *TM*).

9. *"When I am afraid, I will trust in you. In God, whose word I praise, in God I trust; I will not be afraid. What can mortal man do to me?"*
(Psalm 56:3-4, *NIV*).

10. *"Are not two sparrows sold for a penny? Yet not one of them will fall to the ground apart from the will of your Father. And even the very hairs of your head are all numbered. So don't be afraid; you are worth more than many sparrows"*
(Matthew 10:29-31, *NIV*).

11. *"And God is able to make all grace abound to you, so that in all things at all times, having all that you need, you will abound in every good work"*
(2 Corinthians 9:8, *NIV*).

12. *"Cast all your anxiety on him because he cares for you"*
(1 Peter 5:7, *NIV*).

Every Christian has the right to believe that God watches out for him or her. *"When I said, 'My foot is slipping,' your love, O LORD, supported me. When anxiety was great within me, your consolation brought joy to my soul"* (Psalm 94:18-19, *NIV*).

God also has the right to expect His children to show forth to the world around them that they have complete trust and confidence in His goodness and power towards them. Christians must be ready to show that God's people are different—that they trust and expect divine interventions in their lives in these troubled times, unless God has other plans for them. Non-believers are frightened, and we can understand why. They don't know if they might die, and they don't know where they will go if they do die. But why are many Christians terrified of death? As Christians, we must never forget that this is not our home, this is where we are walking out the learning of God's love and His destiny plans and purposes for our lives. Our home is with Him in eternity. *The Message* tells us:

"Friends, this world is not your home, so don't make yourselves cozy in it. Don't indulge your ego at the expense of your soul. Live an exemplary life among the natives so that your actions will refute their prejudices. Then they'll be won over to God's side and be there to

join in the celebration when he arrives. Make the Master proud of you by being good citizens. Respect the authorities, whatever their level; they are God's emissaries for keeping order. It is God's will that by doing good, you might cure the ignorance of the fools who think you're a danger to society. Exercise your freedom by serving God, not by breaking the rules. Treat everyone you meet with dignity. Love your spiritual family. Revere God. Respect the government."

(1 Peter 2:11-17, *TM*)

COURAGE AND COMFORT

Thank you, Lord, for recording in your Word that you did not turn Thomas or Peter away from you when they struggled with doubt and fear. I come to you now for encouragement, strength, and assurance so that I might cease my struggles. I thank you for this moment of rest in the present tense of your love today. Right now, the past is over and the future is not yet–you are my present-tense, right-now God.

I bind myself to your timing for all things. I bind my mind to the mind of Christ, expecting an infilling of His thoughts and peace. I loose all wrong patterns of thinking that would try to set themselves against such an infilling. I loose all worries and anxieties over what has happened before and what will happen next.

To be comforted means to be soothed, consoled, reassured, calmed, relieved, and put at ease. We feel comforted when we are supported, encouraged, and strengthened. How comforting it is to also know that God has accepted us as we are, especially when we feel we may never step up to the Joshuas, the Deborahs, the Rahabs, the Peters, and the Pauls of the Bible. By His grace and mercy and our own cooperation, we will continue to grow into our destinies. Grace and mercy is the highest form of comfort the human soul can know. Grace and mercy soothe, console, calm, and strengthen us.

"Is anyone crying for help? God is listening, ready to rescue you. If your heart is broken, you'll find God right there; if you're kicked in the gut, he'll

help you catch your breath. Disciples so often get into trouble, still, God is there every time. He's your bodyguard"
(Psalm 34:17-20, *TM*).

I recently read a small plaque in a discount store that said, "It is better to be kind than to be right." How simple, yet profound! Kindness looks beyond whatever self-validation "being right" would bring, and projects goodness and genuine caring towards others. The more sure people are of their worth to God and their identity in Christ, the less important it is to them to "be right." God and His angelic forces may be our bodyguards, but we hold the commission of kindness to help comfort the souls of our fellow man.

Biological Warfare

Most Americans have managed to deny the possibility of biological warfare on our home ground. But it is truly a frightening thing to consider if you believe you are the final source of your own protection. How do you personally protect yourself against the threat of poison in the mail, poison in the water, or in buildings where you work? Many newspaper journalists and television newscasters have eagerly reported every piece of information they could get their hands on about potential biological poisons (such as anthrax) being unleashed upon America. But government officials have tried to assure America that the potential problem is really very small. Who do we believe? We all need to take a deep breath, confess that our help will come only from God, and thank Him for giving divine guidance to the men and women who are working to avert such an emergency.

What a comfort our guiding God is! Jesus told His disciples, just prior to ascending into heaven to sit at the right hand of the Father, that, *"Whoever believes and is baptized will be saved, but whoever does not believe will be condemned. And these signs will accompany those who believe . . . when they drink deadly poison, it will not hurt them at all . . ."* (Mark 16:16-18, *NIV*). Barnes' Notes on the Bible tell us that the use of the term "any deadly thing (*KJV* wording)" means anything poisonous that usually causes death.[4] Believers need to know that they can trust God to keep such deadly poisons from hurting them. Faith is our shield against such works of our enemy.

As the anthrax threat became real, some people immediately began trying to buy up and hoard the antibiotics that were supposed to cure anthrax poisoning. Others have stockpiled weapons, food, and water. I remember years ago, perhaps in the mid to late 1970s, when several spiritual leaders were advising people to store up grain and other food stuffs in large barrels for the hard times that were soon coming. I wonder how much of that grain eventually got moldy and mildewed, but was never eaten?

What people need now is not just an antidote for anthrax and whatever type of biological warfare might be thought up and released against America. They need the antidote that comes from faith (trust and confidence) in God's promises in His Word. You cannot prepare for every evil plan that might come your way, but God can.

When I was just a fledgling bank employee, about to become a teller at the age of 19, I was told that I would be charged back with any counterfeit bills that I accepted. I was very nervous and worried, asking everyone I worked with to show me what counterfeit bills looked like. No one told me what they looked like or showed me any counterfeit bills. They just put me on the vault teller's station where I counted and banded money all day long, five days a week, for several weeks prior to going on the actual teller line. I became so familiar with what real money looked like, I immediately spotted a counterfeit bill when it came over my counter. The only thing we can have right now that is guaranteed to give us the protection we need against whatever evil thing twisted minds might think up, is to become extremely familiar with the Real Thing. We need to be so familiar with the power and promises of God that we automatically reject anything else.

God is the vaccine, the all-purpose inoculation against the deadly things of fear, murderous hatred, chemical warfare, and the other frightening elements of today. Some might say that it is impossible for us to be protected with an all-encompassing antidote or vaccine against such things. The word impossible really only means human beings don't know how to make it happen. With God, nothing is impossible!

"Impossible" is only true when it applies to human-based knowledge, which is why all things are possible with God–He is never limited to our knowledge. Human knowledge is finite. It has a beginning and an end, caused by the human mind's ability to process only known data. The human mind cannot process data it has no knowledge of. God knows everything, however.

The all-encompassing vaccine against chemical warfare is the power of God, explained and outlined in the Word of God—His instructions, His promises, His guidance. Perhaps you feel you have tried His Word already. Did you really, or did you read a verse for the day out of a devotional? You do not get inoculated against disease by having a large, leather-bound container of the vaccine sitting on your coffee table. You do not get cured of a biological disease by holding antibiotic pills in your hand or packing them under your arm. You must open up the container of the vaccine or antidote and consume its contents. How much faith do you really have in the power of the Word to protect you? A truthful answer will be directly related to the amount of the Word you have consumed.

As stated before, the word *faith* as used in the Bible actually means to have trust and confidence in God's goodness towards you. We all have faith in something. The atheists' faith is in their belief that there is no God. Think about that. They must have a lot of faith in that belief to take a chance on ticking off the Creator of the universe and beyond! The

Satanists' faith is in their belief that Satan is the only true source of power. Think of the faith they have to have to believe that Satan is more powerful than the God who bounced him out of heaven for trying to take over. In the year 1999, believers and non-believers put a great deal of faith into believing and preparing for the great crash that the Y2K scare predicted.

We have so often placed faith in the wrong things. The terrorists' attacks have proven that the best of our best leaders, when operating in their human abilities, were not able to prevent the tragedy that occurred. Only God could have prevented it, and we had pretty well shoved God out of our way. America needs leaders in every phase of the national government, every state government, every city government, who know how to pray and seek the face of God for the unknown data, the supernatural information that only His infinite thinking can provide for us.

One bright light of hope that Americans have right now is a Christian president who knows how to do that. Now, we must pray for those leaders who do not know how to submit their planning and strategizing to the one Expert who can guide us through these perilous times.

"So do not worry, saying, What shall we eat? or What shall we drink? or What shall we wear? For the pagans run after all these things and your heavenly Father knows that you need them. But seek first his kingdom and his righteousness (Seek the Real Thing), *and all these* (other) *things will be given to you as well"*

(Matthew 6:31-33, *NIV*).

The next wonderful passage is just too **comforting** to shorten. Read this three times a day as if it were your prescription bottle of truth and faith. God's Word has supernatural power to comfort and encourage:

"Then Jesus said to his disciples: 'Therefore I tell you, do not worry about your life, what you will eat; or about your body, what you will wear. Life is more than food, and the body more than clothes. Consider the ravens: They do not sow or reap, they have no storeroom or barn; yet God feeds them. And how much more valuable you are than birds! Who of you by worrying can add a single hour to his life? Since you cannot do this

very little thing, why do you worry about the rest? Consider how the lilies grow. They do not labor or spin. Yet I tell you, not even Solomon in all his splendor was dressed like one of these. If that is how God clothes the grass of the field, which is here today, and tomorrow is thrown into the fire, how much more will he clothe you, O you of little faith! And do not set your heart on what you will eat or drink; do not worry about it. For the pagan world runs after all such things, and your Father knows that you need them. But seek his kingdom, and these things will be given to you as well. Do not be afraid, little flock, for your Father has been pleased to give you the kingdom'"

(Luke 12:22-32, *NIV*).

Fear of Death

Because of the incredible number of horror movies, slasher movies, monster movies, witchcraft and vampire television programs, and more, many people today have no idea how much darkness they have allowed to accumulate in their souls. What have we done to our children's minds that are not capable of separating reality from fantasy, by letting them feed on these terrible images and wicked story lines? Many adults have no idea of the incredible amount of darkness they have taken into their own souls. Such darkness really messes up our reality checks on truth or fiction.

Fear of death has caused many to be overwhelmed with uncontrollable thoughts of terror and panic. Non-believers fear death because they have no idea of what will happen to them after they die. I hope many American believers have realized how fragile their trust in God really was, and how quickly it evaporated when the menace of death hovered around them. This has definitely been a warning of how little of the truth of the Word resides in some of us. No one wants to be separated from their loved ones, of course, but to be terrified by death is not reasonable when you are a Christian. Death means that we are absent from the body here and present with the Lord there (2 Corinthians 5:6). What a trade off!

Paul was very excited when he spoke to the Corinthian Christians, reaffirming their security in Christ Jesus. He frequently faced very hard circumstances, with his life often being at risk for Jesus' sake! Yet Paul said:

"The things we see now are here today, gone tomorrow. But the things we can't see now will last forever. For instance, we know that when these bodies of ours are taken down like tents and folded away, they will be replaced by resurrection bodies in heaven—God-made, not handmade—and we'll never have to relocate our 'tents' again. Sometimes we can hardly wait to move— and so we cry out in frustration. Compared to what's coming, living conditions around here seem like a stopover in an unfurnished shack, and we're tired of it! We've been given a glimpse of the real thing, our true home, our resurrection bodies!"

(2 Corinthians 4:18-5:5, *TM*).

"Therefore we are always confident and know that as long as we are at home in the body we are away from the Lord. We live by faith, not by sight. We are confident, I say, and would prefer to be away from the body and at home with the Lord. So we make it our goal to please him, whether we are at home in the body or away from it"

(2 Corinthians 5:6-9, *NIV*).

All that we have now is perishable, just as stored grain only maintains its value and goodness for so long and then it rots away. If we are trusting in God, placing all of our confidence in Him, and He chooses to have us be with Him, we have gained our next home in eternity. Consider what Paul called a "mystery":

"Listen, I tell you a mystery: We will not all sleep, but we will all be changed—in a flash, in the twinkling of an eye, at the last trumpet. For the trumpet will sound, the dead will be raised imperishable, and we will be changed. For the perishable must clothe itself with the imperishable, and the mortal with immortality. When the perishable has been clothed with the imperishable, and the mortal with immortality, then the saying that is written will come true: Death has been swallowed up in victory. Where, O death, is your victory? Where, O death, is your sting?"

(1 Corinthians 15:51-55, *NIV*).

Praying For Others

Father, pour out your healing upon those who are mourning for lost loved ones. Please ease their pain and grief with your love. Reassure them that those who died in this tragedy were not alone when they took their last breath—that Jesus was with each one of them. No one sat alone in any of the seats on the destroyed airliners. Jesus spoke with each one whether they knew Him or not. He offered them love, comfort, peace, and the opportunity to know Him. The people who collapsed in smoke-filled stairwells, unable to go any further— Jesus sat with them to the moment of their final breath, encouraging and comforting them.

The pilots, the flight attendants, the passengers, the people who worked in the buildings, the firemen, the chaplains, the policemen, the Christians, and the non-believers who were killed—not one of them died alone. Each one of them realized Jesus was with them before they died. Each one of them had the chance to take His hand and step into eternity with Him. The God who created time can turn an earthly millisecond into an hour of eternal understanding.

Lord, please do not let any religious, legalistic thinking close in on those left behind grieving. Not everyone gets saved at an altar in a church. Some get saved in airplanes, some in dark stairwells, and some in the millisecond before a disastrous event overtakes them.

Be ready to embrace every opportunity to use your gifts in serving and comforting others. Let God help you to serve so that you will always impart His grace in whatever way will be the most effective. Know the Word of God, and know your Lord through prayer and communion. Be able to speak as He would speak to those around you. Don't ever refrain from going to someone who is distressed because you do not know what to say. In fact, do not be afraid to say nothing at all. But be willing to pray, to listen, to touch, or hug. Trust God to give you words if they are necessary. Sometimes just weeping with someone, just listening to someone, or just sitting quietly with someone, can comfort them.

> *"I long to see you so that I may impart to you some spiritual gift to make you strong—that is, that you and I may be mutually encouraged by each other's faith"*
> (Romans 1:11, *NIV*).

Those who offer comfort and encouragement to others often find themselves being blessed and encouraged as well. There is a mutual encouraging that takes place when there is a right agreement of faith, of trust and confidence in the goodness of God. We have been comforted so that we can comfort others and help them receive the peace and the truth of God's love again. The Apostle John said, *"I have no greater joy than to hear that my children walk in truth"* (3 John 1:4 *KJV*). The epistle writers of the New Testament often refer to seeing the peace and truth in others' lives as a source of their personal joy.

> *"Praise be to the God and Father of our Lord Jesus Christ, the Father of compassion and the God of all comfort, who comforts us in all our troubles, so that we can comfort those in any trouble with the comfort we ourselves have received from God. For just as the sufferings of Christ flow over into our lives, so also through Christ our comfort overflows"*
> (2 Corinthians 1:3-5, *NIV*).

What the devil meant for evil, God will turn to good. Knowing this can take the ugly things that have happened in our lives and turn them around. When we realize this same kind of turn around can happen in others' lives, we can become the hands, the hugs, the words of God to help them receive such a miracle.

Something within the human soul rises up to act with heroism and compassion when a major tragedy occurs. But all too often, as the emotional impact of such a tragedy fades, people move back into their own narrow lives. It is wonderful to see all of the giving going on right now, but when there is no money left to give, when there is no more need for blood, then what will people be willing to give? Love, life, and hope are what we are required to give and give and give. The need for an ongoing expression of such things will never stop.

"God is love. When we take up permanent residence in a life of love, we live in God and God lives in us. This way, love has the run of the house, becomes at home and mature in us, so that we're free of worry on Judgment Day—our standing in the world is identical with Christ's. There is no room in love for fear. Well-formed love banishes fear. Since fear is crippling, a fearful life—fear of death, fear of judgment—is one not yet fully formed in love. We, though, are going to love— love and be loved. First we were loved, now we love. He loved us first. If anyone boasts, 'I love God,' and goes right on hating his brother or sister, thinking nothing of it, he is a liar. If he won't love

*the person he can see, how can he love
the God he can't see? The command we
have from Christ is blunt. Loving God
includes loving people. You've got to
love both"*

(1 John 4:17-21, *TM*).

Pray this prayer for people who are
hurting, changing the pronouns as needed, or
changing the focus to pray it with someone
who is hurting:

*Jesus, _____ has lost someone very
dear to him. He feels such pain and grief
in his soul right now. I believe he also
feels overwhelming anger, confusion,
and fear. Anger because his loss seems
so unfair. Confusion because he does
not understand why it happened. Fear
because he doesn't know what else he
might lose. You have said that all things
work together for good for those who
know and love you, but he does not
know what possible good lies in this loss.
Help him to trust you to work it to good.
Help him to surrender his questions to
you and make room to receive your
grace and comfort. He so needs to make*

96

room in his pain and grief for your joy, peace, and comfort.

I bind _____'s mind, will, and emotions to your will. Help him to embrace Christ's assurance in his mind that he will know joy, peace, and hope again. Hold him tight to your will until his life moves beyond this loss.

I loose all thoughts of "if only I had . . . what if I had . . . why didn't I . . . " from _____. I loose denial and hopelessness from his soul. Help him to give his loss to you, choosing to let go, knowing that overcoming his grief and healing will not mean he has forgotten the loved one he has lost. I bind his mind to the truth that overcoming and healing through your strength means he will be able to freely think on the good memories he has without fearing an encounter with unresolved pain. Father, help him to stop from grieving over what could have been. I bind _____, body, soul, and spirit, to your good plans from this point forward in his life.

Lord, help _____ to understand that when a loved one who believed in Christ has died, we know we will see that one again. But there are times when a loved one dies, never having professed belief in Christ as far as anyone knew. We must remember that we have no idea what that person's final words with Jesus were just before death. We have a blessed hope that our prayers for our loved ones caused a softening in their hearts during their final moments for such a talk. Amen.

It can be very hard to comfort someone whose will is set in a completely opposite direction to yours, someone whose temperament is different than yours. We have to learn how to comfort with the comfort of God, rather than trying to comfort only as we would understand and accept it. As you comfort, try to be completely free of any judgment of the grieving person's situation or life. Keep a compassionate expression on your face, never showing any impatience. Be certain that you are willing to accept that a person can be in deep pain and distress whether or not it makes any sense to you. And, never, never react to or take personally what the hurting person says or does.

TURNING BACK TO YOU, LORD

The attack on America has been and is hard for human hearts to process and accept, Father. When this world closes in on me, let me remember to do what Jesus did—slip away and find a quiet place to pray. This is the only true and right response when I'm pushed beyond my finite limits. Help me to know when to reach out and pray with others, as strangers did all over America on September 11, 2001. If my circumstances prevent me from praying aloud during the day, please listen to my heart's quiet prayers for your will to be done.

Help all Americans to understand that money and power cannot guarantee security. Help them to seek first the Kingdom of God, loosing all fear and every doubt about whether or not you will be there for them. I loose all wrong beliefs, wrong teachings, wrong agreements, and wrong patterns of thinking from every person in America. I bind every person in this country to your will. Those who have felt the sting of prejudice or ignorance, those who have experienced strong emotional reactions because of being "different," Lord, I bind their minds to the mind of Christ. I loose the effects and influences of the negative agreements they have entered into with each other regarding the source of their pain.

Father, show us how to always pray in agreement for the one result that is always right: <u>That your will would be done on earth as you have so set it in heaven</u>. You have chosen us to be the instruments of what you want to *manifest on earth. What an awesome responsibility you have entrusted us with and how we have fallen short of fulfilling it up until now. I will change!*

What Satan meant for evil, Lord turn it to good. Let there be a great spiritual revival come from this tragedy, that many would come to know Jesus Christ as their Savior and Lord.

The book of Nehemiah is considered by some to be the book of the Comforter, the Holy Spirit. Nehemiah means "Jehovah consoles" or "comforted of God" or "God is consolation," depending upon which resource books are referenced. Nehemiah was deeply troubled over the desolation of his nation and longed to console and comfort his fellow Israelites. He prayed (Nehemiah 1:4-11) day and night in intercession for his country. He confessed both his individual sin and his country's national sin, pleading with God to remember His promises of mercy upon their turning back to Him, <u>regardless of how far they had moved away from Him</u>.

Nehemiah always beseeched God to remember that these were His people redeemed by His strong hand, reminding Him that His honor was at stake in their situation. Nehemiah, Ezra, and Daniel all prayed these same kinds of prayers for their nations. Where are the people today who will pray with passion and weeping over this country, asking God to forgive both their own sins and the sins of their fellow Americans? **This is the price that Americans may not be willing to pay for their land to be healed.**

In the time of Nehemiah's great distress, the walls of God's holy city, Jerusalem, were broken down and the gates were in ruin. The city's enemies were able to come and go as they pleased. This deeply grieved Nehemiah when he learned of it, and the Word says he fell into a flood of sorrowful weeping for days. He poured out his soul to God. He came before the Father with a holy confidence in His loving grace, certain that He would keep His covenant and extend mercy to those who needed Him. Nehemiah was convinced of this, even though God's people had rebelled and turned away from Him. Nothing is too much to ask God for when you believe in His promises to rescue and restore those who have stumbled off in the wrong direction.

In Nehemiah's prayer, as in Daniel's prayer (Daniel 9) and Ezra's prayer (Ezra 9), he confessed that his nation had sinned against

God, and that he and his father's house had sinned against God as well. He humbled himself before God, he prayed with deep sorrow, he sought His face (he pleaded for, desired, and inquired of a personal hearing before God). He committed himself to turn from his wicked ways (he repented and committed himself to turn away from former ways and change).

Nehemiah quoted God's own words to remind Him (although He needs no remembrance) that He had said if His people would turn back to Him, He would gather them to himself again. Our very best prayers are grounded in the promises of God; the promises of the Word that give us great cause to hope for healing and restoration. We have the right to hope that as our fellow Americans turn to Him, He will gather them to himself.

When Nehemiah had completed his prayers for help for his country, he did not sit back then and say, "God has to do something now. I've done my part." Nehemiah backed up his faith with action. He began to cooperate with the instructions he received from God and rebuilt the walls of Jerusalem. Sometimes God restores supernaturally, and sometimes He uses His people to restore that which has been torn apart and destroyed.

In Isaiah 45:18-19, we can read how God says He formed the earth to be inhabited, and those He created to inhabit the earth were not called to a fruitless service. They would receive a just reward. The *Amplified Bible* gives a very strong statement in verse 19 of God saying that He was speaking about this in righteousness and truth. *"I, the Lord speak righteousness—the truth, trustworthy, straightforward correspondence between deeds and words."*

Our prayers at this time must be prayed with a straightforward correspondence between the words we have prayed and the ensuing deeds that we do. If we pray and ask God to restore our nation, then we must be ready to help in the process if He opens a door for us to do so. If we pray and remind God of how good He is, how powerful He is, and how filled with love and mercy He is—then we must act like we absolutely believe He is.

> *"Words are not mere words, you know. If they're not backed by a godly life, they accumulate as poison in the soul"*
> (2 Timothy 2:16, *TM*).

God spoke to Isaiah, as He now speaks to us as well, saying, *"Do not fear, for I am with you; do not be dismayed, for I am your God. I will strengthen you and help you; I will uphold you with my righteous right hand. All who rage against you will surely be ashamed and disgraced; those who oppose you will be as nothing and perish. Though you search for your enemies, you will not find them. Those who wage war against you will be as nothing at all. For I am the LORD, your God, who takes hold of your right hand and says to you, Do not fear; I will help you"* (Isaiah 41:10-13, *NIV*).

Ephesians 2:10 in the *Amplified Bible* speaks very clearly of how we are not spiritual accidents in the Kingdom of God, rather our very lives are God's own workmanship. We were recreated in Christ Jesus, even born anew, to fulfill great works, walk great paths, living out a good life. It seems so incredible that these things were preordained for us before we were even born, but God has always had a plan for our lives. Nothing done to us, nothing we have done, and nothing that has happened in these times changes that. Our God, and His love for us, is the same yesterday, today, and tomorrow.

As soon as we are willing to recognize and accept this, we can begin to travel on

God's "tracks" that He has laid down for us to follow. We will never be aware of these "tracks" as long as we do not believe they exist for us.

> *"God made my life complete when I placed all the pieces before him. When I got my act together, he gave me a fresh start. Now I'm alert to God's ways; I don't take God for granted. Every day I review the ways he works; I try not to miss a trick. I feel put back together, and I'm watching my step. God rewrote the text of my life when I opened the book of my heart to his eyes"*
> (Psalm 18:20-24, *TM*).

> *"What a stack of blessing you have piled up for those who worship you, ready and waiting for all who run to you to escape an unkind world"*
> (Psalm 31:18, *TM*).

I received the following by e-mail about two weeks after the attack. I have no idea who wrote it, but these simple comparisons caused me to pause and consider the changing of all of our priorities.

On Monday, there were people fighting against praying in schools.
On Tuesday, it was hard to find a school where someone was not praying.

On Monday, people were fighting each other because of race, sex, color, and gender.
On Tuesday, they were all holding hands.

On Monday, people were fighting against the Ten Commandments on government property.
On Tuesday, the same people said, "God help us all."

On Monday, politicians argued about budget surpluses.
On Tuesday, grief stricken, they sang "God Bless America."

On Monday, people were upset that commuter traffic made them ten minutes late.
On Tuesday, they stood in line for hours to give blood for the dying.

On Monday, some children had families.
On Tuesday, they were orphans.

On Monday, we e-mailed jokes.
On Tuesday, we did not.

I realized that on Monday, September 11, 2001, I had been irritated at a neighbor for occasionally walking across my private deck. On Tuesday, I realized how absurd my irritation seemed. I realized that thousands of my fellow Americans would never walk across any deck again, and how I would have given my deck, my home, and more to return that privilege to them. We cannot change what has happened, but we can change what might yet happen by our faithfulness in prayer. Let us be Daniels, Nehemiahs, and Ezras. Let us be life-changers.

I pray that you *"being rooted and established in love, may have power, together with all the saints, to grasp how wide and long and high and deep is the love of Christ, and to know this love that surpasses knowledge—that you may be filled to the measure of all the fullness of God"* (Ephesians 3:17-19, *NIV*).

ENDNOTES

1 Marshall, Alfred. *Interlinear New Testament*. Grand Rapids, MI: Zondervan, 1975.

2 *Matthew Henry's Commentary on the Whole Bible:* New Modern Edition, CD-ROM, Hendrickson Publishers, Inc., 1991.

3 *Adam Clark's Commentary*, CD-ROM, Biblesoft, 1996.

4 *Barnes Notes,* CD-ROM, Biblesoft, 1997.